Baking Soda

Discover The Incredible Health, Personal Hygiene, And Cleaning Hacks That Everyone Needs To Know About Baking Soda

Written By

Ashley Stone

Ashley Stone

This document is geared towards providing exact and reliable information in regards to the topic and issue covered. The publication is sold with the idea that the publisher is not required to render accounting, officially permitted, or otherwise, qualified services. If advice is necessary, legal or professional, a practiced individual in the profession should be ordered.

- From a Declaration of Principles which was accepted and approved equally by a Committee of the American Bar Association and a Committee of Publishers and Associations.

The information provided herein is stated to be truthful and consistent, in that any liability, in terms of inattention or otherwise, by any usage or abuse of any policies, processes, or directions contained within is the solitary and utter responsibility of the recipient reader. Under no circumstances will any legal responsibility or blame be held against the publisher for any reparation, damages, or monetary loss due to the information herein, either directly or indirectly.

Respective authors own all copyrights not held by the publisher.

The information herein is offered for informational purposes solely, and is universal as so. The presentation of the information is without contract or any type of guarantee assurance.

The trademarks that are used are without any consent, and the publication of the trademark is without permission or backing by the trademark owner. All trademarks and brands within this book are for clarifying purposes only and are the owned by the owners themselves, not affiliated with this document.

Table of Contents

Introduction

I want to thank you and congratulate you for getting the book, "Brilliant Baking Soda".

This book contains proven steps and strategies on how to use this traditional (and often overlooked) substance for much more than baking! Covering cleaning, hygiene and health, this book will teach you the money saving benefits of using Baking Soda to clean just about everything (and everyone) in your home.

Thanks again for getting this book, I hope you enjoy it!

Chapter 1
Old Wives (and Grandma's) Tales

Baking Soda; we've nearly all heard of it and most of us have some lurking at the back of a cupboard in the kitchen. For those who bake regularly it will be a familiar item, regularly used and much loved! For others it could be one of those mysterious substances that sits in the cupboard largely unused until a recipe calls for a pinch or two.

Yes, Baking Soda is an essential ingredient in all manner of baked goods from cakes and cookies to breads and muffins. A simple, plain and inexpensive white powder it's essential in baking but that's about it. Isn't it? Well, not exactly. Some people may well have that box or container in the cupboard but also keep a little in the refrigerator. An old wives' tale, possibly your own old grandma's tale, suggesting that it keeps things fresh and reduces odors. However, when grandma starts suggesting you can use that innocuous looking powder to treat itches, to freshen up the dog's breath or even to fight fires, you might be forgiven for thinking that Grandma is becoming confused.

Wrong; old wives (and grandma's in particular) tend to know a thing or two when it comes to frugal housekeeping tips. Baking Soda can be used for an astounding range of household cleaning, culinary and even medicinal uses. It's cheap, widely available and sadly overlooked in our modern world. Thanks to the needs of large, commercial organizations, who need mainly to make a profit, Baking Soda has been replaced by many exciting, far more expensive products in many of its traditional uses. However, for those of us who like to keep the costs down, or simply avoid using too many dangerous chemicals when cleaning our homes, Baking Soda can provide a perfect alternative.

Baking Soda is, in fact, a very powerful little chemical agent. "Chemical" sounds bad but actually, in this case at least, it's a safe one. More accurately known as bicarbonate of soda, it occurs naturally and is by-product of the mineral Natron. Often found in natural springs where Natron is present, the chemical is produced through natural reactions with air and water. The powdery, crystalline form found in nature has also long been used by man, and woman, as a cleaning agent. Long, in this case, stretches right back to the days of ancient Egypt. Yes, even in those ancient palace kitchens, there were little boxes of Baking Soda, lurking at the back of cupboards! In fact, the Egyptians appear to have used the powder more as a cleansing agent – which is just one of its many uses.

Ashley Stone

One of the big advantages of Baking Soda over commercially available cleaning products is that it is non-toxic, which means it's also environmentally friendly. The non-toxic part is likely to be of interest to those with small children, who are naturally inquisitive. Cleaning products produced by many firms are highly toxic and when little, inquisitive hands work out how to access them, disaster could be not very far away. As an alternative to toxic-chemical rich cleaning products, Baking Soda has a lot to recommend it!

But the fun doesn't stop there, when it comes to Baking Soda. The chemical is also produced, naturally, by the body to regulate acidity in the stomach and the blood. The man-made alternative has also long been used in a medical setting to help reduce indigestion and stomach acid.

While many of us may have forgotten (or never heard of) the many and varied uses that the humble Baking Soda can be put to it hasn't been entirely forgotten in some industrial processes. Bicarbonate of soda can be used to remove paint and is particularly good at removing paint from metals which may be damaged by more acidic substances.

Baking Soda is a slightly alkaline substance which helps to neutralize acids (hence its effectiveness at reducing stomach acid). This is also the reason that it is effective at neutralizing bad smells and odors. In the refrigerator, for example, a smell of sour milk, caused by the decomposition and release of acids will be easy to remove using Baking Soda, which simply reacts with the acids and neutralizes them.

In terms of cleaning, Baking Soda is not just effective but it's very adaptable to different circumstances (this is what makes it so flexible). If you're faced with a greasy pan, for example, add some Baking Soda; it reacts with the fats in grease and effectively turns into soap! As the basic form of Baking Soda is crystalline it can also be used as an effective scourer; simply add a touch to a sponge and wipe! Unlike some commercial scouring agents the crystals are fine enough to make an effective scourer that doesn't scratch, making it perfect for delicate surfaces around the home. To make a basic cleaning paste all you need to add is water; this makes a good cleaning "product" to clean off surfaces and tiles.

Added to any normal soap, Baking Soda will increase the effectiveness of the soap. Another old trick is to mix Baking Soda and vinegar together; this creates a bubbling, effervescent mixture which lifts dirt off just about any surface. Baking Soda can even be used to douse small kitchen fires. This is only recommended for grease based fires and also works on electrical ones (Baking Soda is used in fire extinguishers!). Simple smother the flames with Baking Soda and problem solved. Remember this should only be used on small fires, on the hob, to stop the flames. Also remember to never tackle any fire unless you are certain that you can bring in under control quickly.

Medical uses for bicarbonate of soda have long been implemented. Today a surprising number of medicines actually contain "Baking Soda", more likely found on the ingredients as bicarbonate of soda and it's also commonly found in toothpastes. Apart from commercial medicines you can use Baking Soda for a number of home remedies and we'll look at these later in the book.

While you may have a small box or container of Baking Soda in the cupboard, you may be surprised to find that it's commonly found in somewhat larger quantities on many farms. It's used in commercial cattle feed to reduce stomach acid in cattle! In dairy herds this promotes milk production and in beef herds it has the effect of reducing acid, increasing food intake and thereby maintaining a higher body weight.

Last but not least, of course, Baking Soda can be used in baking! By reacting with acids in milk, yogurts and other ingredients the soda forms bubbles which are then trapped within the protein gluten causing the mixture to rise. Baking Soda? Overlooked? Just a little!

Basic Applications for Baking Soda

There are four simple ways in which you can apply Baking Soda for a range of household applications. These are:

- As a paste, roughly 1 part water to 3 of Baking Soda.

- Dry, simply sprinkled

- In the box, for deodorizing simply remove the lid.

- As a solution, roughly 4 tablespoons to a quarter of a pint of warm water.

Note the use of "roughly" here; there's no need to be absolutely exact when using Baking Soda for cleaning purposes. This doesn't, however, apply for medical applications, where you'll need to be more careful with amounts and we will look more closely at this later in the book.

Chapter 2
Baking Soda in the Kitchen

Baking Soda is incredibly flexible and adaptable when it comes to cleaning and you might be surprised at the number of products (of the expensive variety) that you can substitute with Baking Soda. As it's likely that the standard issue half-forgotten box of Baking Soda is in your kitchen we may as well start with some common kitchen cleaning applications for Baking Soda!

Odorless Refrigerators

In most kitchens, at some point or another, a forgotten food item will be found lurking in the refrigerator. It happens to the best of us! Even with the offending item removed, the smell can linger. Simply place a box or container of Baking Soda at the back of the refrigerator to eliminate the unpleasant smell. You can leave a box filled with Baking Soda in the refrigerator as a permanent fixture but you'll need to replace the supply every few months. You can pour the used Baking Soda down the drain as it's perfectly safe for the environment and it'll freshen up your kitchen drain on the way - wash it down with vinegar to create additional de-greasing and cleaning power.

Garbage Odor Neutralizer

Simply sprinkle Baking Soda at the bottom of the trash can before placing a bag in the can. This will effectively neutralize odors for several weeks but it's worth wiping old Soda out once a week and refreshing with new.

Cookers, Grills and Ovens

Quickly sprinkle Baking Soda on a damp sponge and wipe; this should effectively clean off bits of difficult to remove food, grease and grime. Once everything is bright and shiny again, rinse off with warm water and leave to dry.

Microwave Miracles

Microwaves are great but they're often found with bits of food determinedly clinging to their oven walls! Place 2 tablespoons of Baking Soda in a cup and fill with warm water, give it a quick stir and the place in the microwave. Boil this for two minutes and remove; stains and stuck on food will now easily wipe away!

Everything, including the Kitchen Sink

For a gentle, ex-foliating scrub for your kitchen sink, sprinkle some Baking Soda around the sink and then add drops of vinegar. The vinegar/Baking Soda mix will bubble away nicely and you can scrub this round with a scrubbing brush before rinsing away with water. This is particularly useful for delicate stainless steel and will clean extremely well, without scratching.

Stronger Scourers

For a more robust scouring mixture – not suitable for delicate surfaces but great on stronger materials – mix salt and Baking Soda together. You can store this mixture in bulk and use as required, applying with a damp cloth or sponge. This works well on ceramic or tile surfaces and splash-backs.

Extreme Washing Up

OK, you don't have to wash up during a bungee jump. In these case we mean extremely powerful washing liquids! Add Baking Soda to your standard liquid or soap and wash up as normal. The strength is up to you but a couple of tablespoons is a basic amount for an extra strength wash. If you use a dishwasher you can sprinkle Baking Soda on the bottom for a deodorizing effect between washes and a little boost during washes.

Pots, pans and Blenders

You may be beginning to realize by now that you can clean most things with Baking Soda! For stubborn pots, pans, coffee makers and blenders Baking Soda is a simple, no hassle cleaning product. For blenders mix water and Baking

Soda in the bowl and blitz for a 30 seconds. Empty, rinse and dry. For coffee makers simply add a teaspoon to the reservoir and fill with water, run through a cycle or two to clean and deodorize. For stubborn grease and baked on stains in pans or baking trays add 2 tablespoons of Baking Soda, ½ a cup of vinegar and a cup of water. Bring the mixture to the boil in the offending pot/tray and allow to boil for 10 minutes (you'll need some ventilation for the fumes from the vinegar). Finally wash as normal, which should require a lot less scrubbing!

Oven Cleaner

A Baking Soda paste is an effective oven cleaner and far less toxic than the commercial kind. Make a paste with roughly 3 parts Baking Soda to 1 part water. For stubborn grime substitute equal amounts of Baking Soda and Salt. Scrub as usual but if using salt ensure this is thoroughly rinsed to avoid corrosion.

Floor Cleaning

An alternative to chemical cleaning agents can be made with ½ cup of Baking Soda and a bucket of warm water. Mop as usual for a perfect shine. For marks on lino or vinyl floors scrub Baking Soda gently onto the mark with a damp cloth or sponge.

Culinary Tricks and Treats

While you can, and probably do, use Baking Soda in baking, why stop there? There are a number of really helpful ways in which Baking Soda can add (or subtract) from a number of dishes. Here are just a small selection of ideas.

- For omelettes or mashed potatoes with a little extra fluffiness, just add Baking Soda! ½ a teaspoon for every two eggs will create a fluffier lighter omelette texture and just a pinch added to mashed potatoes will make a light, fluffy texture that your friends and family will marvel at.

- Gravy and sauces can often separate when cooking, or left to cool for too long. Simply add a dash of Baking Soda during cooking to bind the fats together and create a smoother sauce or gravy. A dash here means just a little caught between your fingers and stirred in thoroughly. For tomato based sauces, like bolognaise or chili, you can reduce the acidity of the tomatoes by adding just a little Baking Soda – a pinch stirred in well should be enough. This also works in any dish where you've been too enthusiastic with the vinegar – simply add a pinch of Baking Soda to re-balance the taste and acidity.

- If you enjoy cooking game you'll be aware that some meat can be just a little too gamey on occasion. If this seems to be the case simply soak the uncooked meat overnight in water and Baking Soda. This will lighten the flavor. This is great when cooking for guests who may not be used to game dishes.

- As Baking Soda is perfectly safe to eat you can use it as a cleaning agent when preparing fruit or vegetables. Simply scrub fruit and vegetables with water and Baking Soda to help remove dirt, grime and germs.

- If you love coffee but suffer from excess stomach acid you'll most likely be advised to cut caffeine altogether. If this is a sacrifice too far, don't panic. Just a pinch of Baking Soda added to coffee will reduce the acidity of the drink and should help to avoid any side-effects from your morning cup!

Chapter 3
Bathrooms and Baking Soda?

Our bathrooms, like our kitchens, see some of the heaviest daily "traffic". Waste water is not the only thing that goes down the drains from the bathroom, plenty of household cleaning chemicals used in bathrooms also make their way into the sewer. It's probably fair to say that more pollutants escape our bathrooms than any other part of our home. The good news is that Baking Soda is not limited to either baking or using to clean kitchen areas. It makes a powerful and effective alternative in the bathroom too. In this chapter we'll take a tour of the bathroom and see just how useful Baking Soda can be at cutting through dirt, deodorizing and, perhaps most importantly, saving you money on expensive cleaning products.

Bored of the Rings?

Tired of rings around the tub after bathing? Add 2 tablespoons of Baking Soda to your bath and banish them for good. This also has the additional benefit of making the water softer – in hard water areas this is great but it makes for a more pleasant soak whatever the local water quality in your area. The alkaline qualities of Baking Soda can also help to soften the skin and expel toxins from the skin – by neutralizing acids.

Blockage Busters

The water trap just beyond the plug in sinks, baths and showers inevitably becomes blocked over time with grease, hair and grime. To avoid it becoming too blocked you should regularly flush with a cleaning agent and Baking Soda will do the same job as any commercially available product. Use a cup of Baking Soda, combined with a cup of salt and ½ a cup of vinegar. Pour this mixture down the plugs (bath, shower and sink) and leave to stand for around 15-20 minutes. Have your boiling water ready at the end of this time and use it to flush the mixture down the drain. The solution will help clear drains as it goes. Repeat at least once a week for best effects.

Healthy Hair Brushes

To clean hairbrushes and combs simply soak in Baking Soda Solution, a teaspoon in 1 cup of hot water should be enough to loosen any dirt and grime that may have built up, keeping brushes and combs clean and hygienic. You can clean toothbrushes in the same manner by soaking overnight in a solution of Baking Soda.

Toilet Tactics

To clean the toilet with Baking Soda simply throw ½ a cup into the bowl and scour as normal with a toilet brush. If the bowl is stained add ½ a cup of vinegar and scour. In both cases once you've scoured allow 5- 10 minutes for soaking before flushing the mixture away. To clean the water tank simply add a cup of Baking Soda to the tank and leave overnight before flushing through; once a month is ideal but this can be done as often as you like and will keep both the tank and the bowl sparklingly clean.

General Bathroom Cleaning

Safe and, non-abrasive, a damp cloth or sponge with Baking Soda applied can be used to clean down most bathroom surfaces. Wipe round as you would with normal, expensive, potentially toxic chemicals, for a much healthier and environmentally friendly clean! This will work on chrome, porcelain, fiberglass and tiled surfaces or fittings.

Shower Curtains

Shower curtains can become moldy and mildewed over time and plastic ones can simply be washed in the washing machine. Adding Baking Soda along with your normal cleaning detergent will make for a better finish and more hygienic one. Add just ½ a cup and put through a gentle wash cycle for best results.

That Unmentionable Smell

Bathrooms and closets are prone to some unpleasant smells from time to time. You can use standard air fresheners but Baking Soda will neutralize nasty smells just as well. Simply place a bowl on the water tank of the toilet (or behind the toilet) to create a home-spun air freshener. Unlike commercially bought fresheners Baking Soda is not perfumed and is far better if you suffer from allergies or asthma.

Tiles and Grout Grime

Cleaning the grout between tiles and the tiles themselves is best achieved with a Baking Soda paste. Use 3 parts of Soda to 1 part of water for the paste. You can apply the paste to the tiles with a cloth or sponge but for grout between tiles an old toothbrush is ideal. Scrub the tiles and grout thoroughly and then rinse or wipe with a damp cloth. For very stubborn stains you can use bleach instead of water but remember to use gloves and keep the room well ventilated while the bleach is present.

Shower Heads and Doors

Over time sparkling shower heads can become dull and residue can build up around the water outlet. Baking Soda will come to the rescue in this case! You'll need to fill a plastic bag – a strong one is best – with ¼ of a cup of Baking Soda and 1 full cup of vinegar. Tie this so that the shower head is completely immersed in the liquid and leave for at least an hour. The mixture will bubble enthusiastically and remove grime, lime-scale and dirt. Carefully remove the bag and dispose of the mixture down the drain. Dry and polish your now sparkling clean shower head! For a brilliant finish to your shower doors use a spray filled with vinegar. Scour with Baking Soda, using a sponge and finally rinse and dry.

Bathroom Floors

As with the kitchen, an effective and safe cleaning solution can be created using Baking Soda, simply add ½ a cup to your mop bucket and polish to a sparkling finish.

Chapter 4
Laundry Magic

Love it or hate it, laundry has to be done. Baking Soda makes life easier and helps to remove all manner of stubborn stains and difficult dirt. Again, it's cheaper than many of the alternatives and in this chapter we'll look at the uses of Baking Soda in the Laundry Room. Sadly, Baking Soda is not a substitute for standard laundry detergent but it can be combined with (and substituted for) several other laundry liquids.

Liquid Detergent

Although you can't substitute this completely you can make it last longer by adding some Baking Soda. ½ a cup added to liquid detergent will make it stretch and will also produce a better cleaning effect. This only works well with the liquid variety, although Baking Soda with powdered detergents does help to produce extra white whites.

Baking Softener

Forget commercial fabric softeners! Baking Soda can be used instead and it's not only just as effective but much kinder on sensitive skin. This is particularly useful for anyone with allergies or skin conditions such as eczema. It's also a lot softer on your housekeeping budget.

Bleach Solutions

Baking Soda is brilliant at producing, well, brilliant whites. It's best to use some bleach as well but you can cut the amount you would normally use to half and substitute Baking Soda for the rest. Not only does this create those brilliant whites but it's much gentler on fabrics and is especially good for delicate fabric.

Stubborn Stains?

On whites or colored clothes you can create a paste using Baking Soda which will see them off. This works on collars and cuffs too and is a lot better for most fabrics than bleaching and gentler than scrubbing with soap. For cuffs and collars simply make a paste using 3 parts Soda and 1 part white vinegar, apply this and then wash as normal. For tough stains, including sweat, tea, coffee, or grease, make a paste using water rather than vinegar and apply this to the stain but allow it to sit for 30 minutes to an hour before washing. If possible, when it comes to tea, coffee, grease or wine try to catch the stain when it's fresh; rinse quickly with water and then apply a paste of Baking Soda.

Toxic Spills

If you accidentally spill any acidic substance on clothing it will soon wreak havoc. Always rinse the item of clothing straight away and then sprinkle the stained area with Baking Soda. This neutralizes the acid immediately and stops it corroding the fabric. If the acid has already dried it's important to add Baking Soda to the item of clothing before washing to avoid the acid being reactivated in the wash. Common causes of acid stains on clothing include other cleaning fluids (particularly bathroom ones) and battery acid, urine or vomit. Using Baking Soda on stained baby clothing will help to lengthen the life of the clothing and is also softer and safer on delicate young skin.

Dirty Clothes

Most of us have busy enough lives and we can't always wash clothes as quickly as we like. If you have a washing basket full of dirty clothes awaiting your attention, especially if these include dirty sports clothes, simply sprinkle Baking Soda onto the pile to keep the smells at bay. The clothes can be washed when you have time and you don't need to remove the Baking Soda before doing so! Don't be afraid to be liberal with the amounts to get the freshest effect. You can also sprinkle Baking Soda into sneakers to reduce their potency! Shake the sneakers out before wearing.

Swim Wear

Chlorine from the pool soaks into your swim wear and will leave it smelling rather unpleasant – simply soak in a solution of water and Baking Soda. Soak for an hour with about ½ cup of Baking Soda and 4 pints of warm water. Drain away after an hour and the chlorine will be gone! You can then wash as normal.

Iron Cleaners

If you have a steam iron and notice that residues are building up on the base and steam outlets, simply wipe down (when the iron is off) with a damp cloth and Baking Soda. For nozzles or steam outlets use a cotton wool bud dipped in Baking Soda. Residues will be cleared away rapidly, leaving your iron in peak condition.

Litter Freshener

Not strictly a laundry tip but often a cat litter tray is located in the utility room! Sprinkle Baking Soda over the top of the litter to freshen and reduce odors.

Chapter 5
Beyond the Kitchen

Well, beyond the kitchen, bathroom and laundry, to be precise! Baking Soda has a multitude of uses around the home for cleaning and freshening. In this chapter we'll take a tour of the home and we'll be taking our Baking Soda with us.

Upholstery Cleaning

Tired, worn and looking like it's seen better days? Upholstery can be quickly and easily freshened with little effort using Baking Soda. Simply sprinkle over the offending item and allow it to rest for 15 to 20 minutes before vacuuming off. The soda will freshen the appearance but also eliminate unpleasant odors. Ideal if you have small children, pets or husbands.

Cloths, mops, dusters and Rags

Simply rinse and then soak any of the above in a solution of 4 tablespoons of Soda and a quart of water to clean and deodorize. Cloths rags and dusters will be freshened in a short time but mops may need to be soaked over night. Once cleaned and fresh simply leave to dry.

Fire Tiles, Hearths and Brickwork

All of these can easily be cleaned with Soda. Scrub hearths, bricks or tiles around the fire with a solution of 4 tablespoons to a quart of hot water. For stubborn stains apply a paste of 3 parts Soda to 1 part water and allow to sit for 30 minutes prior to using the water solution to scrub. Wipe off any residue once complete for a perfect finish.

Back in the Closet

Keeping odors at bay and to keep clothes fresh you can add Baking Soda to closets and drawers. Although you can sprinkle Soda in the closet a small sachet will be ideal. Simply create one using muslin, or even an unused paper coffee sachet. Replace regularly with a fresh sachet. From time to time, in closets, simply sprinkle the floor, leave over night and vacuum the following day.

Alternative Carpet Cleaning

There are two simple methods to use Baking Soda for effective carpet cleaning. To simply deodorize the carpet, sprinkle plenty of Baking Soda around the room before vacuuming. For best results leave in place for at least fifteen minutes. You can also leave the Baking Soda overnight if you prefer. Baking Soda can also be used to make a simple carpet shampoo; use ½ a cup per gallon in you carpet cleaner instead of commercial shampoo. Check beforehand that your carpet is colorfast by dabbing a solution of soda and water on to an inconspicuous corner as you would with normal shampoo. For stains you can add a sprinkle of Baking Soda to the stain while the carpet is damp. For heavy stains mix Baking Soda and salt in equal parts and brush over the stain. Leave for at least a couple of hours, but preferably overnight, before vacuuming. A thick paste of Baking Soda and water may also remove stains. Apply to the area in question and leave it to dry completely before vacuuming up – again overnight is ideal.

Rust Removal

For small items – nuts, bolts and screws – which are rusty, you can soak in a solution of Baking Soda and vinegar. Sprinkle Baking Soda over them first and then cover in vinegar. The mixture will bubble and leave it to work its magic until the bubbling has stopped.

Smokey Atmospheres

In smoking households ridding yourself of the unpleasant smell of smoke can be easily achieved with a simple home-made deodorizer. Use a spray bottle and fill with 4 tablespoons of Baking Soda and warm water. Spray into the air to remove the smell. You can add Baking Soda to the bottom of ash trays to minimize the smell. Replace each time you empty the ashtray – this method also helps to ensure that cigarettes are extinguished.

The Writing on the Wall

A safe cleaning solution for walls can be made by mixing 1 cup of Baking Soda and a squeeze of washing up liquid to 4 pints of warm water. This wipes down walls and removes stains. If there really is writing on the wall, courtesy of small people armed with crayons, Baking Soda will come to the rescue. Add some to a slightly damp sponge and apply with a moderate amount of elbow grease! Repeat as and when necessary (usually for up to about ten years)!

Gentle Jewelry Cleaning Solutions

Use a mixture of standard soap (a gentle variety) and Baking Soda. You can apply this with a toothbrush or damp cloth to polish jewelry and remove dirt from chinks and crannies in delicate items.

Dog Care with Baking Soda!

You can "dry clean" your dog quickly and effectively by simply sprinkling a little Baking Soda onto their coat, then brushing off. This is a very effective fast deodorizing method. Added to your pet's bath water the Soda will soften both the water and their coat, leaving it soft and shining. If you have a particularly relaxed dog you can also brush their teeth with Baking Soda. This is just as effective as any commercial varieties and is safe for dogs. Pet bedding can be sprinkled with Baking Soda and then shaken or vacuumed. Again this deodorizes and freshens the bedding, eliminating smells. This can be applied to any pet bedding – cat etc. You can also sprinkle Baking Soda at the bottom of animal cages to keep them smelling fresh.

Chapter 6
Health and Hygiene

Baking Soda, or Bicarbonate of Soda, has been used in various medical settings for the last couple of hundred years. Thanks to its unique qualities it has a number of beneficial health and hygiene uses. In this chapter we'll be looking at how Baking Soda can be used in home-made medicines.

Before we start it's important to note that Baking Soda may not be suitable for everybody. If you have hypertension, are on salt-restricted diet, are pregnant or breastfeeding you should check with your doctor before using Baking Soda. Follow the guidelines carefully in this chapter – in previous chapters amounts have been flexible but for health purposes do not use more than the stated amount. Avoid using Baking Soda for medicinal purposes for children under five years old.

Baking Soda Toothpaste

Perhaps one of the oldest uses for Baking Soda – and one where commercial varieties of toothpaste also contain the product. Simply brush your teeth as normal with just a little Baking Soda dabbed on your toothbrush. This will whiten your teeth well. It's important to note that commercial toothpaste contains fluoride and this is recommend for combating cavities (particularly in children) and so Baking Soda alone should not be used as a substitute for toothpaste but as an additional whitener. Dentures can also be soaked in Soda to clean. Use a solution of 2 teaspoons in a small bowl big enough to contain the dentures and leave overnight.

Shaving Lotion

Use 1 tablespoon of Baking Soda mixed with a cup of warm water to moisturize your skin before shaving. This will soften the skin and hair, making shaving easier and it will also reduce post-shaving rashes.

Baking Soda Antacid

Use ½ teaspoon in ½ a glass of water. Drink slowly and do not take another dose for at least two hours. Take no more than 7 doses within 24 hours. Use for no more than two weeks and consult your doctor if symptoms persist.

Burn or Rash Cream

Use this mixture on minor burns or on rashes. Create a paste of 3 parts Baking Soda and 1 part water and apply to the affected area. This should cool and soothe the burn or rash. This is particularly effective on rashes caused by chicken pox or shingles and can provide much needed relief.

Stings

For Bee stings apply the paste described above, for burns or rashes, as quickly as possible. In the case of wasp stings substitute vinegar instead of water and again, apply as quickly as possible. If the sting is still visible try to remove it by brushing or flicking it away.

Athlete's Foot

Often caused by moisture and sweat which encourage fungal infections athlete's foot can be treated with a paste of Baking Soda. A thick paste is best and this can be applied between the toes. Leave for 15 – 20 minutes before rinsing off and drying. By dusting your toes and shoes with Baking Soda you'll also be able to reduce the amount of moisture produced and limit the chances of re-infection.

Blackheads and spots

These can be effectively treated by using a thick paste of Soda and water. Use only a little water to make a stiff paste and apply this to the affected skin. If possible, leave this paste on overnight before washing off thoroughly.

Congestion Relief

For adults only, mix a ¼ of a teaspoon of Baking Soda and 1 tablespoon of water. Once the Soda has dissolved use an eye dropper to drop into the nasal passage. After a few minutes the congestion should be relieved. Repeat as required.

Itchy, sore skin

This can be relieved with a light wash of 1/3 cup of soda and 4 pints of water, simply sponge on to relieve dry itchy skin. This should also work on light sunburn. To soften hard skin on feet, or simply as a softening, refreshing and revitalizing foot-bath, use around 4 tablespoons of Baking Soda and a quart of warm/hot water.

Friendly Deodorant

Simply sprinkle under arms to create a natural alternative to commercial deodorants. Baking Soda neutralizes body odor and it's also more gentle on the skin than many mass-produced products which makes it ideal for those who suffer from skin conditions, allergies or intolerances to the chemicals contained in many stick or spray deodorants.

Nail Cleanser

For dirty or stained nails simply gently brush a little Baking Soda over the tips and surface of the nail. This works on all manner of stains (and cooking smells) and is particularly good at removing dirt from under the finger nails after gardening or DIY. Use a light vinegar wash for stubborn dirt or grease and then rinse thoroughly.

Hairspray Removal

If this has built up rather too much simply add a tablespoon of Baking Soda to your regular shampoo and lather up as normal. The soda will remove any excess hairspray very effectively. Rinse and condition as normal.

Stop Smoking Aid

Not all smokers, but many, will find that Baking Soda helps to reduce nicotine cravings. Mix one tablespoon of soda with a glass of water and drink (slowly) twice a day for the first week of quitting and one glass a day for every week while cravings and urges persist. This doesn't work for everyone but many people do find that it's a simple and effective method to help them to quit.

Mouthwash

Simply add 1 teaspoon of Baking Soda to ½ a cup of water and rinse, gargle but don't swallow. This doesn't just cover up bad odors, it completely neutralizes them!

Conclusion

Thank you again for getting this book!

I hope this book was able to help you to discover some surprising uses for that humble box of Baking Soda lurking at the back of a kitchen cupboard near you!

The next step is to start putting your new found money-saving tricks into action.

Finally, if you enjoyed this book, please take the time to share your thoughts and post a review on Amazon. It'd be greatly appreciated!

Thank you and good luck!

Made in the USA
Columbia, SC
12 September 2023

22791177R00022